MACDONALD
STARTE

Toys

Macdonald Educational

About Macdonald Starters

Macdonald Starters are vocabulary controlled information books for young children. More than ninety per cent of the words in the text will be in the reading vocabulary of the vast majority of young readers. Word and sentence length have also been carefully controlled.

Key new words associated with the topic of each book are repeated with picture explanations in the Starters dictionary at the end. The dictionary can also be used as an index for teaching children to look things up.

Teachers and experts have been consulted on the content and accuracy of the books.

Illustrated by: Michael Ricketts, Ann Ricketts

Editors: Peter Usborne, Su Swallow, Jennifer Vaughan

Reading consultant: Donald Moyle, author of *The Teaching of Reading* and senior lecturer in education at Edge Hill College of Education

Chairman, teacher advisory panel: F. F. Blackwell, general inspector for schools, London Borough of Croydon, with responsibility for primary education

Teacher panel: Elizabeth Wray, Loveday Harmer, Lynda Snowdon, Joy West

© Macdonald and Company (Publishers) Limited 1972
Third Impression 1974
Made and printed in Great Britain by Purnell & Sons Limited
Paulton, Somerset

ISBN 0 356 03997 8
First published 1972 by Macdonald Educational
St Giles House
49-50 Poland Street
London W1

We are getting all our toys
out of the toy box.

I have lots of toy cars.
Some are made of plastic.
Some are made of metal.

Some of my toys are made of wood.
These bricks are made of wood.

3

These toys float in water.
They are fun to play with
in the bath.

4

My sister often plays with dolls.
She is bathing her dolls.

Many toys are made in factories.
This is a factory
for making dolls.

Machines make all the parts
of the dolls' bodies.
The parts are made of plastic.

These girls are painting
eyebrows and lips on the faces.
A machine puts on the hair.

These girls fix
all the parts of the dolls together.
They dress the dolls.

Here are some dolls from many countries.
People collect these dolls.

This is one of Great-grandma's dolls.
It is made of china.

Toy soldiers were made
of metal or wood.

12

Here is a pedal car.
It looks like a real car.

This toy crane
can really lift things.
14

I made this kite.
It flies high in the air.

These children
are playing in the park.
They are sailing toy boats.
16

This toy aeroplane
is made of balsa wood.
Some toy aeroplanes
can glide through the air.

Here are some puppets.
You wear them on your hands.
They are called glove puppets.
18

These puppets are different.
They have strings fixed to them.
You pull the strings
to make the puppets move.

It is easy to make toys.
Here are some of the things
you can use to make toys.
20

cork chicken

stocking doll

potato elephant

handkerchief
parachute

21

back   front

Some people like to make
toy animals.
They make them out of cloth.
22

Starter's **Toys** words

toy box
(page 1)

car
(page 2)

wood
(page 3)

bricks
(page 3)

float
(page 4)

water
(page 4)

bath
(page 4)

sister
(page 5)

doll
(page 5)

factory
(page 6)

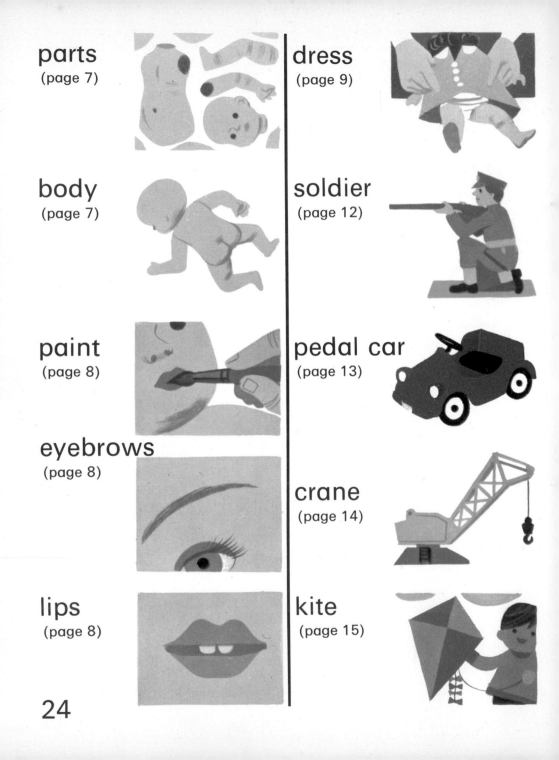

parts
(page 7)

body
(page 7)

paint
(page 8)

eyebrows
(page 8)

lips
(page 8)

dress
(page 9)

soldier
(page 12)

pedal car
(page 13)

crane
(page 14)

kite
(page 15)

fly
(page 15)

glide
(page 17)

children
(page 16)

hand
(page 18)

park
(page 16)

glove
puppet
(page 18)

boat
(page 16)

string
(page 19)

aeroplane
(page 17)

toy animal
(page 22)

25